What pec

Finding Zen in the Ordinary

It is easy to say, "live in the moment." But what does this really mean? The beauty and the power of Christopher Keevil's *Finding Zen in the Ordinary* is its ability to awaken in a reader the felt immediacy of what it is like to be fully present to the world, to ourselves, and to others. This deeply honest sharing by a seeker both passionate and humble will enrich the personal paths—both spiritual and worldly—of other seekers, as it has mine.

David I. Rome, author of *Your Body Knows the Answer: Using Your Felt Sense to Solve Problems, Effect Change, and Liberate Creativity* (Shambhala)

Author Christopher Keevil likens his book to an arbor of spiritual inquiry where forty-eight koan-like stories and moments of insight and enlightenment lie on its branches. He offers this arbor not as a guide but more as an inspiration for our own spiritual inquiry and longings. He's a wonderful companion to have at your side.

Sharon Salzberg, bestselling author of *Lovingkindness* (Shambhala) and *Real Happiness* (Workman Publishing)

In *Finding Zen in the Ordinary*, Christopher Keevil reveals glimpses of the extraordinary that is the ordinary nature of the world, if our minds were just quiet enough to see it. With deeply honest reflections, koans and stories, he gives life to the three kayas: the plane of possibility; deep appreciation; and acting with wholeness with a voice that is uniquely his, revealing worlds within worlds.

Jonathan F.P. Rose, author of *The Well-Tempered City* (HarperOne); Co-Founder, Garrison Institute; Founder, Jonathan Rose Companies

Finding Zen in the Ordinary is an accessible, wise and winsome invitation to the philosophy and practice of Zen Buddhism, enriched with signposts for further exploration. Insightful, thought-provoking and delightful.

The Rev. Caroline M. Stacey, Rector, *Church of St. Luke in the Fields*, New York City

Finding Zen in the Ordinary is a rare encounter with the fruits of deep reflection and spiritual inquiry. In the immediacy, tenderness, and wisdom of his Zen stories and poems, Christopher Keevil has captured the surprises, rewards, and challenges of a life committed to "just being with what is." This book is a wonderfully fresh and clear-eyed sharing of life on and off the cushion, a companion for beginners and old practitioners alike.

Robyn Brentano, former Executive Director of *The Tibet Fund* and the *Garrison Institute*

Finding Zen in the Ordinary

Stories and Reflections

Finding Zen in the Ordinary

Stories and Reflections

Christopher Keevil

MANTRA
BOOKS

Winchester, UK
Washington, USA

JOHN HUNT PUBLISHING

First published by Mantra Books, 2021
Mantra Books is an imprint of John Hunt Publishing Ltd., No. 3 East Street, Alresford
Hampshire SO24 9EE, UK
office@jhpbooks.com
www.johnhuntpublishing.com
www.mantra-books.net

For distributor details and how to order please visit the 'Ordering' section on our website.

Text copyright: Christopher Keevil 2019

ISBN: 978 1 78904 449 2
978 1 78904 450 8 (ebook)
Library of Congress Control Number: 2019945258

A CIP catalogue record for this book is available from the British Library.

Design: Stuart Davies

UK: Printed and bound by CPI Group (UK) Ltd, Croydon, CR0 4YY
Printed in North America by CPI GPS partners

We operate a distinctive and ethical publishing philosophy in
all areas of our business, from our global network of authors to
production and worldwide distribution.

Contents

In some stories, names have been changed to preserve anonymity. Names of Zen teachers and historical figures are unchanged.

A sesame bun, as pictured on the cover, alludes to the exchange at the end of Chapter 28.

Foreword

Dìzàng asked Fǎyǎn, "Where are you going?"

Fǎyǎn said, "Around on pilgrimage."

Dìzàng said, "What are you on pilgrimage for?"

Fǎyǎn said, "I don't know."

Dìzàng said, "Not knowing is nearest."

—Case 20, Book of Serenity

Chris has studied Zen with me for nearly three decades. The pilgrimage of our lives has been filled with many Zen retreats and countless face-to-face meetings, phone dialogues, and written inquiries. Our intention has always been to deepen and clarify our understanding of the immediacy of present-tense experience. In this process our appreciation of the vast silent mystery that is our life reveals itself. It is here that the deep comes to the surface in the moments of everyday life. As the renowned Zen Master Dogen said, "The whole world is mind ground, the whole world is blossom heart."

Of the many shared experiences Chris and I have had over the years, some stand out because they have a holographic quality and are reminders that the whole is revealed in each of the particulars of our lives. As the Heart Sutra proclaims, "Form does not differ from emptiness, emptiness does not differ from form." Essential nature and its phenomenal expression are always one.

In the 1990s, Chris attended a weeklong Zen retreat that I led on a ranch deep in the wilderness of the Carson National Forest in New Mexico. Nestled among the old-growth Ponderosa pines we sat and melted into the mountains, supported by visitations from elk and bear, and the chorus of wild birds.

After a week of intense formal practice, it was the custom to share a cup of tea. Each member of the sangha was also encouraged to present a short comment or gesture that revealed a moment of immediacy that stood out during the retreat.

This kind of sharing as an expression of the koan of our lives is greatly revered in the Zen tradition. The less that is said, the better — a picture is worth a thousand words. A simple gesture or phrase can reveal the true meaning of koan as "truth happening place."

The Zen stick was passed around the sharing circle so that each person had the opportunity to present some living truth from the week of silent sitting. When the stick arrived in Chris's hand, he lifted up his tea cup and poured warm tea over his head. Laughter and tears filled the hall. Just this.

The vignettes and teachings of *Finding Zen in the Ordinary* are compelling because they are expressions of the warm heart and clear mind of compassion and understanding. A vignette is a short evocative account of everyday life. It is also a photographic technique, in which a small illustration or portrait is shaded gradually at the edges, which leaves no definite line or boundary between foreground and background. The portraits of this collection are the particulars of a person's life: "Walking through the Chapel Square Mall" or "Leader of the Choir." The background or common denominator of them all is the essential nature that permeates all of life. "Buddha nature pervades the whole universe, revealing itself right here, right now."

It is my hope that the stories and teachings of this book will inspire the reader to grow in love and understanding. May they inspire each of us in our own unique way to go forward in service of alleviating the suffering of our troubled world.

Zen Master Bo Mun
(George Bowman)
August 2018

Introduction

I came to Zen one evening at the Cambridge Insight Meditation Center outside of Boston. At the end of the group meditation someone announced that Baghdad had just been bombed by U.S. warplanes. It was the beginning of the First Gulf War.

I didn't know the international affairs behind the action, but I felt the weight of my country's involvement in such human suffering.

A guest speaker got up in front. He was from the Cambridge Buddhist Association across town. "My heart is in my mouth," he said. "I came here to give a talk, but hearing of the bombing, all I can do is to lead us in chanting." There was a moment of stillness. Some of the people got up and left, but many of us stayed.

So we chanted. We chanted to Kanzeon, the bodhisattva who hears the sufferings of the world. Our guest speaker stood in front, tapping a woodblock to keep the rhythm. His voice was strong and unassuming. He had a remarkable ordinariness.

Drawn to this teacher, I began attending Wednesday-evening meditation sessions at the Cambridge Buddhist Association. We alternated 30-minute periods of seated meditation with 10-minute periods of walking meditation. During one of the periods of sitting, the teacher, whose name I had learned was George Bowman (Zen Master Bo Mun), would give a talk. Later in the evening, he would hold one-on-one meetings where we would receive Zen stories and sayings to contemplate. He would challenge and encourage us.

My study with George has continued over many years. We have sat in meditation together. We have chanted together. We have shared anguish and laughter.

This book offers an arbor of spiritual inquiry that has been nurtured through this relationship and has been growing throughout my life. On its branches lie forty-eight pieces; discoveries arising from the ordinary. There are stories, prose poems, essays, and dialogues.

Additional resources are provided after the forty-eight pieces, including Zen Master Bo Mun's ten principles of Zen along with tables that correlate the forty-eight pieces with the ten principles. These are followed by endnotes which offer commentary, references and definitions.

This book is more of a companion than a guide. It recounts events and moments which have strengthened my intent to live from a place of honesty and lovingkindness. It offers a way of finding Zen in the ordinary.

Christopher Keevil
October 2018

1. 4:30 a.m.

Stillness.

Cross-legged on a cushion,
only the faint light of a distant streetlamp
on the wall.

Now settling in,
breathing slow, mind wide open:
the calm surface of a moonlit lake.

Little thoughts ripple
then subside.
All is vast and quiet.

A question emerges.
What am I doing here?
Is there a playbook for this show?

All that replies
is a great stillness
with the quality of a question mark.

―――――

―――――――――

――――――

――

2. In the Subway

This morning I'm in a crowded subway car on the way to a meeting. The car jerks and squeals, smelling of steel and spots of old chewing gum. Zen practice: just being with what is.

Then, an unexpected commotion. Several feet away, a tall youth with messed-up hair and jerking eyes is swearing, now louder. He looks about to pick a fight.

A space opens up as people back away in the crowded car. Things could go badly. Is there something I can do?

A man standing close by with graying hair and muscular shoulders leans over to the fellow and says, "Hey man, you're going to be OK, you'll be OK," his voice deep and full of care.

The youth looks up; his face relaxes. He turns away, muttering. The subway car breathes a sigh of relief. And I realize, as my balance returns, that my question has just been answered.

———

3. When the Engine Stops

Airplanes fascinated me as a young boy. Appearing from behind the trees they would advance overhead, roaring or growling, then disappear again into silence. Sometimes they stayed behind our tall backyard trees or hid in the clouds. Then my ears would find and follow them.

Near my home was a small regional airfield. All sorts of aircraft took off from there—single-engine planes, twin-engine planes, small jet aircraft, helicopters, even the Goodyear Blimp on wonderful and rare occasions. The throaty whine of the blimp's engine would get me and my siblings rushing outside hoping for a glimpse.

Of all the aircraft sounds, one was most curious. It would start with the nasal hum of a single-engine plane high overhead, then go entirely silent for a while. Eventually it would start again, all in mid-flight. This would occur on weekend afternoons when the weather was nice. What was that sound? Likely a flight-training maneuver; some flight instructors will shut off the engine while airborne to teach recovery from an engine failure in flight.

When the engine stopped mid-flight, was there a student in a moment of panic, high in the air? Keep the airspeed up! Avoid a stall!

Times in my daily life are like this.

A client sends an email, "Your presentation yesterday was a disappointment to my staff." My belly stiffens. Blankness and despondency block me as I try to reply.

My teenage daughter wants a ride to a friend's house. I'm just home, exhausted from the day. The urge to rest and the urge to help collide.

Coming out of the drugstore, my left rear tire is flat. For a moment I can't comprehend how to carry on.

When such moments arrive, can I keep my airspeed up and avoid a stall?

---

4. I Choose This

So often, what I am doing is not what I choose.

While talking with an acquaintance at a party
my eyes wander:
is there someone else across the room
I should be talking to instead?

When work appears impossible,
other jobs seem better.
I could be an exercise trainer
or just a stay-at-home dad.

Even in fleeting moments,
while waking up or driving,
I wonder if I should have risen earlier
or taken a different route.

I have spent many years
second-guessing
the here and now.
It's a loss.

Just choose this here and now—
choose this route; this time for rising;
choose this job with its particularities;
choose this person as the one I want to know.

*　　*　　*

A monk asked his teacher, "In summer it's oppressively hot, in winter it's bitingly cold. When hot or cold come, how can I avoid them?" The teacher said, "Why don't you go where there is no hot or cold?" The student said, "Really? Where is that?" The teacher replied, "When it is hot, be killed by the heat. When it is cold, be killed by the cold."

---

5. Red Geranium

What is the present moment?

The past is ungraspable—it's gone. The future is ungraspable—it hasn't arrived. What about the present? Can I grasp it?

Well, how long does it last? Does it have duration? It would seem not. Any duration would mean that past and future are part of the present. But they're not the present. So the present moment is without duration. Without duration, how can it exist?

But it does exist. It's tangible, and palpable ... with an eternal quality. This moment has always been here—it has never left.

Time moves through and past this moment. Every thing rotates by: with glacial slowness, with firecracker speed, or at the pace of walking. And there's this moment, without time.

As I come downstairs, the red geranium sits on the kitchen table, the morning sun fills the air.

* * *

A monk met an old woman on the road and asked if he could buy refreshments from her. She said, "What do you have in that backpack?" The monk replied, "These are commentaries on the *Diamond Sutra*." The old woman said, "In that scripture it says, 'the past mind cannot be grasped, the present mind cannot be grasped, the future mind cannot be grasped.' Which mind are you going to refresh?"

—————

6. When the Door Opened

Tony, a friend of mine, got hit by a bus while walking on a sidewalk in upstate New York. He spent weeks in the hospital healing from internal injuries and broken bones. Once he had recovered enough to walk, he was discharged.

At the time, Tony had no money, no job, and no home. He headed back to New York City where he had lived prior to the accident. He was still recovering and in a lot of pain.

A friend offered a room in his apartment where Tony could stay. The friend, who worked as a mover, was away often on long-distance jobs.

In the top drawer of the bedside table, Tony's friend left take-out menus; the bottom drawer he filled with money—so Tony could order food whenever he wanted.

After some weeks, when the two of them were together in the apartment, Tony's friend told him, "We need to go out." "I can't," said Tony. "I'm hurting all over. I don't want to see anyone."

"That's exactly why we need to go out," said Tony's friend.

"But I don't have any pants," said Tony, who had only the hospital pants he had received after his injury.

"There's a bag of clothing in the corner," said Tony's friend. He walked over and dragged the bag toward Tony. "Find something in here."

Tony tugged an old pair of jeans out of the bag and laboriously pulled them on. Finally, he buttoned the waistband with a grunt, tucked in his shirt and was dressed to go. Together, Tony and his friend went out to the elevator foyer. "Push the button," said Tony's friend, wanting Tony to take the initiative—so Tony pushed the elevator button.

When the door opened, a man with crutches and only one leg was standing there. The man smiled. Tony gasped. He looked hard at the man, then said "How do you do?" The man smiled again, and said, "Come on in."

Tony and his friend stepped forward into the elevator.

Together they all rode down to the lobby and went out the front door of the apartment building. The man with one leg went swinging off down the street with his crutches. Tony said, "Let's go over to the garden at Hudson and Barrow. They've got nice tulips this time of year."

---

7. Why Do You Meditate?

Me: *(Speaking to my Zen teacher)* George, why do you meditate? What brings you to put your whole life into this Zen practice?

George: You know, Chris, for me this life practice continues to be the most challenging and gratifying thing. It requires tremendous curiosity, faith, and courage. It is not for the faint of heart. And in the end, it has no practical value whatsoever. It has no value to the mind that seeks an agenda. It has no value to the mind of comparison.

And yet, and yet ... there is such truth value. Outside my window the morning sky is clear blue. I hear a bird singing above the rooftop of my cabin.

Me: George, recently you said to me that you have a "greediness for enlightenment." What did you mean by that?

George: I have a great longing, a yearning, an aspiration to immerse myself in this study more deeply, and to share my great love with others. Having tasted it, the longing is very great. I don't get tired of it; it endlessly reinvents itself. I want to enlist my resources to say, at the end of the week, at the end of my life, that I had a really good run at it.

Me: I know that feeling. This work we do is so important. I sit each morning; I talk with you every week. I put my heart into it. Even so, the process is mysterious, and uncomfortable.

George: What is the discomfort?

Me: I often feel tentative, and worry that I'm falling short. Working in the garden, I see all the weeds that need pulling. Answering my emails, I fear that the words will come out wrong. Practicing Zen, I'm sure there's more I could do. Is it ever enough?

George: When you look at your whole life by any conventional standards, you are enormously successful. Yet your mind tells you all kinds of stories—and in fact, they're not true. Like me, I've sat fifty years of retreats; I've counseled hundreds of people.

But my mind says, "You can't do it." This happens often just before I give a talk. Then, I give the talk, and it's one of the most generative, joyful things I do.

They appear irreconcilable, the feeling that it's never enough, and yet "doing it" so beautifully. This not-enough-mind seems to come up no matter what we do. Yet when I dissolve my small mind and enter into the moment, I'm amazed by the beauty of it.

So, I am resolved to practice with great humility, and to find "it" when I'm convinced that "it" is not there.

---

8. Today

Waking before sunrise,
I see the news that our president proposes
a major increase in nuclear weapons capability.

Gripping dread.
Images flash of Hiroshima's suffering:
blistered bodies, houses flattened for miles.

Then, stepping out the back door just before dawn,
a luminous moon and one brilliant star
fill the sky.

How will I live today?

9. Distant Temple Bell

Early in my practice, George asked, "How can you stop the sound of a distant temple bell?"

Days of daily meditation passed, going into the question. Block my ears? Wrap the bell's clapper with a cloth? Clearly these weren't the answers the question was after. What was it?

Sounds were continuously arising: the rustle of breath through my nostrils, the swish of car tires on the road outside, the rhythmic drip from the gutter after the evening rain. The flow was endless, unstoppable.

Resting in a river of the endless and unstoppable. At rest in the sound of a temple bell.

Later, George asked, "How can you stop the sound of a distant temple bell?"

"Bong ..."

10. Going to the Still Center

When I am so angry I cannot speak,
I vow with all beings
to go to the still center of the anger
and meet its rawness.

There, a meat claw is ripping at my heart and vitals.
My friend Charlie
asks, "What's wrong?"
I ask him to sit beside me.

"Yes, I see," he says,
looking at what perpetrated the pain.
I begin
to breathe again.

Later Sarah the CEO calls,
"I know you were in a tough spot," she says.
"I didn't mean
for it to happen."

I see the tough spot
she was in as well.
And realize, the Board Chair's statements towards me
weren't personal.

I don't know what I'll say to the Board Chair
when we meet next,
but the way will appear.
My anger has passed.

11. The Winner and the Loser

Once when traveling in Ireland and attending music festivals, I watched a competition of young accordion players. Each player presented their best before a panel of judges.

One of the players, a British man, played with rippling dexterity, but the judges disqualified him before he was done. He cursed quietly as he came off the stage.

It wasn't clear why he had been disqualified. A fellow next to me said, "His musical style wasn't Irish. He didn't get the grace notes right." Another person remarked, "No, it's just because he's a Brit."

Later, in a common room where lunch was being served, the accordionist was sitting with a friend. "What a pisser," said the friend. "You were the best one up there." "I know," said the accordionist, looking down at his hands.

Across the room, the winner was standing amid a group of admirers. "You were brilliant," said a girl twirling her hair. A boy said, "You're the King." Everyone laughed.

Nearby, a man with worn work shoes saw me looking at the scene and smiled. "Isn't it like that," he said.

*   *   *

The monks at a monastery assembled to listen to their teacher's lecture. The teacher pointed at the bamboo blinds, implying they should be opened, as usual, for the talk. Two monks stepped forward and rolled up the blinds. The teacher said,

"One gain, one loss."

---

12. Is It Possible?

Me: George, in your view is it possible for someone to become enlightened, to "wake up?" Buddha said he woke up; and Dōgen Zenji wrote, after traveling to China, "I have resolved the Great Matter." Can this happen for regular people?

George: In my experience there are times when the mind and body fall away and everything is as clear as the noonday sun. This perfection resolves the question of life and death. Yet over my years of sitting, one thing I can count on—this activity never fixates its position.

Me: So, it's not possible to wake up "for good?"

George: Like all of life, the clarity shape-shifts. The observing self separates, admiring its beloved, becoming unclear and searching outside itself ... until a new clarity is manifest with a deeper and clearer resolution. Again, this breaks apart, manifesting a great sense of loss, sadness, and grief. The root and the blossom of the lotus seem to be two sides of one thing.

Thus we find enlightenment as active participation in loss. There is great love, and great sadness. The stakes are high. We care tremendously and it will all be over soon. It pierces the heart and lets us appreciate "life in the form of" in myriad ways.

Me: Have you had awakening experiences that changed you, and you didn't go back?

George: Yes, I have had awakening experiences that

profoundly changed my whole life, and I didn't revert. Yet I still live with frustrations, worry, doubt—and I ask why I am feeling this way, and doubt my realization. And yet, right in the middle of the broken heart is something of enormous beauty. The gist of Zen is cutting the distance and entering into this so deeply that there is no room for opinion. And then it is to *manifest* in more and more situations in life.

13. Buddha, the Window Washer

While I was talking with George this morning, he opened a door for me to this, the other shore.

We were on the phone, I in a Manhattan coffee shop, he sitting in his parked car in Clay City, Kentucky, taking a break between errands downtown.

As we talked, he was watching a man across the parking lot washing windows. "The most profound love arises ..." George quoted from the sutras. "That man, washing windows ... there he is. There's the Buddha. It's no big deal, but it's true."

Upon hearing these words, the whole world imploded. The struggle of *me* versus *them* dissolved. Personality had no boundaries. A great conflagration of truth raged about and within. This continued throughout the day, yet I functioned fully, leading five client meetings one after the other across New York City.

That evening, I gave a presentation to the trustees of a museum, a formal affair. I looked over my notes meticulously before the meeting. Then, as I stood in front of the assembled group, my voice resounded forth with heartfelt passion and energy. I wondered, am I too much, am I coming on too strong? I felt naked and vulnerable, acting from just this truth, my truth, the only truth I have.

After my presentation, the chair of the board shook my hand vigorously, saying, "That was wonderful. Before, I saw you as just a consultant, but this evening I could tell that you were one of us."

---

14. Who Is This Someone?

This evening I am flying from LaGuardia to Buffalo for a client meeting tomorrow. Done with work for the day, I turn to the story in which a Zen teacher asks his students, "Even Buddha is a servant of someone. Who is this someone?"

I sit quietly and wait. Slowly, responses arise:

This someone ... is the one who feels the gentle flow of breath going in and out of these two nostrils.

... is the one hearing the rush of air on the outside of this plane fuselage.

... is the one with no gap between this moment and a story about this moment.

... is the one with no judgment about this moment, with no judgment about having a judgment.

... is the one who rings clear as a bell when struck by life's imperative.

... is the one who needs no words to speak, whose words speak of their own accord.

... is blood, bones, mucus, and muscle, in a miraculous presentation of vitality, no one knows how.

In truth, there is no gap between the question and the answer: This someone is the one asking.

A short while later, the plane touches down and we disembark. Just walking through the Jetway, headed for the hotel.

15. Jock Strap

In high school I played on the varsity soccer team. The team had a custom that had developed over the years. On the bus ride home from an away game when our team had won, a few of the tough boys would descend on one of the weaker team members and, reaching into his pants, physically rip his jock strap off. They would then hold it up in the air with a yell of victory. Or they might stuff it into the victim's mouth, telling him to "eat it." Other boys would look away, or give a nervous laugh. The coach, who always rode in the front seat would sit just facing forward.

One evening as we were riding home on the bus after a winning game, three of the boys came down the aisle, looking for a victim. They started to move toward a boy sitting across the aisle who was something of a misfit, and whom they often ridiculed. Without thinking, I stood up in the aisle to face them and blurted out, "If you're going to rip anyone's jock strap, rip off mine." My chest felt tight. The boys moved closer. "You mother fucker," said one, bringing his face up to mine. My scalp prickled. Then he looked down, and the boys turned and went back to their seats.

When the bus arrived back at our school's parking lot, the coach stood up and said that no one was going to rip off anyone's jock strap any more.

Just this year, I received a call unexpectedly from a man in California. He said he was a therapist. A client had told a story about his high school soccer team, and how a fellow teammate had stood up for him when his jock strap was about to be ripped off. The therapist had gotten his client's permission to call me and say how much it had meant to him.

16. When Will It Come?

A moment of deep realization,
heaven and earth coming together as one

arrives of its own accord.

Invitations can be offered,
conditions can be arranged:
active study, diligent practice, work with a teacher.

It arrives, however,
in its own time
separate from my yearning.

Just as each evening,
I brush my teeth and get into bed.
Sleep occurs of its own accord.

* * *

Kyōgen was asked by his teacher, "Where do you go after you have died?" Kyōgen searched all the scriptures but could not find an answer. In frustration, Kyōgen demanded that his teacher tell him the answer, but his teacher refused. Kyōgen grabbed his teacher, threatening to kill him, but his teacher laughed, saying, "Do you think the answer will come from my dead body?"

Ashamed, Kyōgen apologized and left the monastery, giving up on his hope to find the answer to his teacher's question. After wandering for a long time, he came to an untended tomb of a once-well-known Zen teacher, and settled there, keeping the grounds and receiving an occasional pilgrim.

One day, as he was sweeping the grounds, a pebble swept by his broom hit a bamboo trunk with a "clink." Suddenly the answer to his teacher's question became entirely clear.

17. Hotel Room

Sitting to meditate before dawn:
hot summer morning;
cheap hotel room in Buffalo, New York.

The room is muggy without the noisy air conditioner.
Outside, a trash truck clatters and whines
as it lifts a dumpster in the parking lot.

Then stillness settles in. Breathing slows.
Gazing at the faded brown and green carpet,
the faint hiss of silence in my inner ear.

Yearning is gone.
Concepts are gone.
Thought ripples pass by like occasional birds.

Then, nothing at all ...
No body, no thought.
Wide open space.

Aware.

18. Stages or No Stages?

Are there stages along a path toward enlightenment? I've heard many answers:

(a) Yes, there are stages of growth toward enlightenment.

The Flower Ornament Scripture describes ten stages a practitioner must go through. Ten stages are also depicted in the *Lankavatara Sutra* and the *Surangama Sutra*. And the *Ten Ox-herding Pictures* liken one's object of spiritual seeking to an ox, and shows how one advances through the stages of searching for, catching and taming the ox, transcending both self and ox, reaching the source, and finally returning to the hurly-burly of life.

Do these stages apply to my own life? Perhaps. I feel less reactive and more stable than I used to. I am hopefully more considerate toward others.

(b) Enlightenment happens outside of stages.

The *Heart Sutra* says there is "no path," and "no attainment, with nothing to attain," yet adds, "All buddhas attain full, unexcelled awakening," a paradoxical combination that points to attainment of non-attainment. The Zen teacher Dae Gak reflected that awakening can only happen now, in this moment, not at some point in the future. The only way to awaken is to awaken right now.

(c) Spiritual growth is a helix.

Looking over my notes across the years, the same themes keep arising—the desire to gain, the fear of failure, comparison of myself to others, a hope that spiritual practice will alleviate my suffering. It's very humbling, and it's not clear if I'm advancing spiritually, or if so, in what way.

George says spiritual growth is like a helix. We keep returning to the same areas of work, but each time it's a bit different.

(d) Becoming enlightened is extremely rare.

While enlightenment is possible for everyone, and many people experience transient moments of great awareness, only several people in an eon achieve full enlightenment. Ken Wilbur, a spiritual pundit expresses this view, as did Charlotte Joko Beck, who was a Zen teacher in San Diego. It's unreasonable for me to expect enlightenment in this lifetime. It takes many, many lifetimes to reach full enlightenment, and even then, it's not clear if or when it would occur.

(e) Spiritual realization is loss, not gain.

Realization, enlightenment, involves loss. Concepts, judgments, and expectations lose their hold on me. All hope that something will magically fix my life is lost. The current situation, whatever it is, is what it is, nothing more. From how I typically think about growth—the growth of a tree, or the growth of a business—"spiritual growth" is an oxymoron. As I grow spiritually, I increasingly lose.

(f) Being concerned about my own spiritual growth is a form of narcissism.

True spiritual growth leads to a loosening of the attachment to self, to "me" and "mine," and to being increasingly helpful to other people and all beings. The bodhisattva precepts taken by Zen initiates emphasize selfless action and care for others. If I fret about my own spiritual growth, I am preoccupied by my self, and therefore going away from spiritual realization.

(g) There is no enlightenment toward which to grow.

People I have known who have engaged deep and long in spiritual practice may be unexpectedly kind, or penetratingly insightful. But there are others I know who are kind and insightful, yet not engaged in spiritual practice. And what about the spiritual teachers who have acted with sexual impropriety or greed? Perhaps the idea of enlightenment, of waking up, is just a human, conceptual construction, good for inspiring followers. Perhaps this process of becoming less reactive and more stable is simply the result of maturation and aging, not brought about through spiritual practice.

(h) I can't know.

Maybe these questions cannot be answered. *The Diamond Sutra*, a core Buddhist text, recognizes that no person can ever say, "I am enlightened," because this person would thus partake of the idea of an ego-entity or a separated individuality, and therefore not be enlightened.
Dogen, the founder of the Soto Zen School in Japan, wrote that a person who is enlightened may not know they are enlightened. And George says, "The mind that asks the question cannot know the answer."

Additionally, the only yardstick I can really apply to spiritual growth is my own personal experience. And if I am changing over time, then the yardstick is changing and can't be used as a tool of measurement.

(i) We are all awakened together.

At the time of his great awakening, Buddha sat all night long and was assaulted by demons, temptations, and fears. He persevered, and a vast peace emerged. Then, in the early morning hours, he touched the earth and said, "I and all beings awaken simultaneously." When we wake up, we all wake up.

(j) Stop thinking and practice.

The question will not be answered by the thinking mind. The only way to wake up, to know enlightenment, is to experience it directly. Engage in spiritual practice. See what happens.

Aargh ... So many answers. Which one is right?

It's late. I'll wash the dishes.
Can you sweep the floor?

_____
_____
_____
___

19. Why Not? Because He Didn't

Excruciating failure at the tennis tournament.
Ten of us boys traveled by bus to another camp,
where my brother had been the champion the year before.
I lost my first match and sat around all day
watching others.

I swung back the little brass door
of my college mailbox

and opened the envelope with my semester grades.
C+ in Genetics, a course required for pre-med.
My doctor father had hoped I would succeed.

Again, searing failure this morning.
A client calls.
They are done with our services.
Due to their disappointment,
they are canceling our project two months early.

Sitting in meditation,
I investigate the anatomy of the pain.
Nails and pegs are pulled out;
life's careful construction tumbled
into disarray.

Slowly, the fog of despair disperses,
there is a sort of vibrancy
in the heart of disappointment,
and a sense of humor twinkling
in the crevices of loss.

A feeling arrives,
tender and expansive:
the awkward beauty of this one life.

Yet, I so wanted to win,
to make the grade,
to keep the job.

*   *   *

A monk asked his teacher, "Why did Daitsû Chishō Buddha,
who sat in meditation for ten eons, not attain buddhahood?"

The teacher said, "Your question is self-explanatory." The monk, not understanding, asked again, "He meditated for so long, why couldn't he become a buddha?" The teacher replied, "Because he did not become a buddha."

20. The Question

An ant, vigorously investigating my desktop, stops to clean his antennae, using his forelegs to wipe them attentively, first one, then the other. He pauses, surveying his surroundings, then dashes forward again, zigzagging left and right across my desk.

Does he ever wonder, in his own tiny way, "Why am I here?" Like the time not long ago when I was standing at the foot of my father's bed, his intellect mostly gone from radiation treatments to his brain. He smiled beautifully, but could only muster a quiet "Hello." What is any of us doing here, given that we each crumble in our own time?

This question has propelled me since I was young as I zigzagged through different professions (carpenter, performing artist, advisor to organizations) and wandered through different spiritual inquiries (Quakerism, yoga, Zen). I avoided the question for a time with dogma (leaving college for a Christian cult), and with protocol (in the corporate world where we only needed to solve for the bottom line). But always it returned.

Why so much searching?

Isn't it clear by now?

The answer … is the question.
Why … am … I … here …?
Exactly.

Just hold the question, yearn for an answer, know it is unanswerable and engage wholeheartedly all the same.

And still the question propels me forward.
Like the ant.

*   *   *

A monk asked Jōshū, "Why did the first patriarch of Zen come here from India?" Jōshū replied, "The oak tree in the garden."

---

21. A Place to Stay

The summer I traveled to Ireland was to attend music festivals and hear Irish music. I was just out of college, had little money, and made few plans.

The first night I found a crowded youth hostel in the city of Cork. The mattress sagged and the room smelled of mouse urine. It took a while to fall asleep.

The next morning I walked to the outskirts of town and started hitchhiking, headed for the Killarney Folkfest. I waited a long time, then got a few short rides. Around noon I was standing at an empty crossroads with fields in all directions. Not a car was in sight.

Then a small brown van expanded into view. My hope rose. The van stopped. In the front were two red-haired men. I climbed in the back and we started off. A few minutes later, the driver pointed to his gas gauge. "I'm out of petrol," he said, "You got any money to help pay?" "Sure," I said, handing him a 10-pound note.

A moment later the driver pulled over. "I just remembered we've got to get home," he said. "Sorry." They dropped me by the side of the road, turned around, and left. I stood there feeling dazed.

I walked the rest of the afternoon. By evening I reached a bed and breakfast where the proprietor stared at me. "I've got an unfinished room in the attic," he said. "One hundred pounds. That's the going rate."

The next morning a truck blowing black smoke picked me up. The driver was taciturn. He listened to my stories of the brown van and the bed and breakfast. Letting me off in Killarney he said, "Don't trust everyone you meet."

I figured I should find a place to stay before the day wore on. Posters were everywhere for the music festival—and lodging was all booked. I kept hunting, and took the main road out of town, passing three rooming houses, all with "no vacancy" signs. I walked on, worried.

Coming around a corner, I found a man sitting on the grass, wearing a flannel shirt and hiking pants. He was tying on his shoes. "Hello there," he said.

His name was Lenny. He was from Kentucky. He loved Irish music too, and was here attending music festivals. "Where you staying?" he said. "Dunno," I said. "Everywhere is full."

Lenny paused a minute. "Would you like to borrow this?" he asked, pointing to the tent pitched beside him on the lawn. "It's nice. I'm returning to the States this evening. You can mail it back to me once you're home."

"Really?" I asked, amazed.

"Of course," he said, "Please use it."

Lenny went on to tell me that a year prior he had contracted Guillain-Barré syndrome. In a matter of weeks, he had become progressively more paralyzed until he could move only his eye muscles. He lay in a hospital bed, trapped in his body, unable to move or speak, with a hole cut in his neck for air.

Then, over a series of months he slowly regained control of his body. Now, his only remaining symptom was a slight weakness in his arms. "You can see the scar here," he said, pointing to his throat where the tracheostomy had been.

"When I was paralyzed, I had no idea if I would get better," continued Lenny. "I panicked. Then I got really depressed. But slowly I started to see what matters most. A peacefulness grew in me, and now all I want is to be kind and generous to others. It's become my life."

We parted that day and never saw each other again. I used his tent as I traveled across Ireland—always with a place to stay.

22. On Retreat

Entering the temple with a bow to golden Buddha,
I take a seat on my cushion, cross-legged.
The bell rings, silence overtakes the hall.

Twenty-one practitioners,
earnest, mostly in black robes,
together dipping our oars in the stream and pulling hard.

Eyes open, lids soft, gazing forty-five degrees down.
The polished cherry-wood floor:
lovely, supporting us all.

The mind,
first a snow globe of thoughts,
grows more still.
An occasional swirl kicks up then passes out of sight.

Ahhhhh ... Immense space, vast and boundless.
Radiance, emanating from every thing,
both inside and without.

Hair grows; stomachs growl.
Wood is oxidizing, dust is settling;
everything, everything is in motion.

Legs hurting now from immobility,
willpower comes to hold
the utter stillness for the group.

Finally, the bell rings, the sitting time is over.
A wash of gratitude and wonder carries forth,
as we bow and rise.

23. I Didn't Think It Would Be Like This

My friend Angie has lived for years with her boyfriend. Every so often we meet for tea. "Should I stay with him?" she asks, digging her fork into her paper napkin.

My friend Alan wanted to be an English professor. But he gave in to his father's plan and became a doctor. He had a large house in the country, raised three children, and put them through college. Hidden in his eyes is an unrequited yearning.

My friend Deirdre has a grown son who is schizophrenic. He gets angry often, can't hold a job, and lives a homeless life. He resents her help, but she still offers.

And Margaret had post-partum depression after her third child and never came out of it. She walks a knife-edge and has been hospitalized often.

Yet again, Angie's wide smile and chuckling laugh heal my heart. Alan's unbounded eyes see beauty unexpected, so I see it too. Deirdre offers words of kindness and appreciation every time we meet. And Margaret sends the most caring emails which guide me towards humility, and acceptance.

*   *   *

A Buddhist story tells of a man who was walking across a field, when a tiger appeared and started to chase him. He approached a cliff at the edge of the field and, grabbing a vine, jumped over. Hanging by the vine, he saw the tiger above him. In the gully below, another tiger looked up at him. A little mouse began gnawing at the vine. Then, he saw a strawberry growing nearby. He reached out and picked it. How delicious!

---

24. Ordinary Mind

A Zen teacher was asked by his student, "What is the way?" The teacher replied, "Ordinary mind is the way."

But what is ordinary mind?

Is it in the anguish of toes stubbed against the bedpost this morning?

Or in the ticklish anticipation when dahlia bulbs planted two weeks ago are sprouting with vigor after yesterday's spring rain?

Perhaps it's there when receiving a call from my son and agreeing with no second thought to co-sign his rental agreement for a cautious landlord?

Or when sliding behind the wheel and putting the key in the ignition without looking?

Agnes would laugh if she knew I was looking for ordinary mind. Stop looking. Just be ordinary.

But is looking for ordinary mind ... ordinary mind too?

*   *   *

In our chanting to Kanzeon the Bodhisattva of compassion we say, "This thought comes from Buddha-mind, this thought is one with Buddha-mind."

Stop!

This text is no text.

These

are

eyes

no

eyes.

What??

Shhhhh …

What is there when there is
only "What?"

26.Kindness

Years ago, I was consulting to a manufacturing plant in Worcester, Massachusetts. At the plant they made industrial valves, such as those used to regulate flow in large water pipes.

The manufacturer wanted to reduce errors in the process. I was working with a team of employees to achieve this.

One of the men on the team would always get the extra chair when someone arrived late. He would reach for a pile of napkins if someone spilled their coffee. He would ask team members to say more, to make sure he understood. He was a beacon of kindness and humility.

One day during lunch break in the cafeteria, I sat down across from him and we fell into conversation. We learned where each other lived, and what we did on weekends. After several minutes, I took a leap and told him I was touched by his way of kindness. Had he always been that way, or had something in his life caused it?

The man reflected for a moment, then said, "I changed after the death of my son. You remember the Lockerbie bombing? My son was on that flight. All 259 people on board were killed."

He continued, "After that, I was so sad, and so very angry. It was eating me alive. So I started a support group with parents of those who had been lost on the flight. That helped. Over time, my grief changed to compassion—for the parents, for their children, and for the bombers too."

For years I had wondered if any real people were enlightened. I left the plant that day feeling I had met one.

27. Before and After

From: Christopher Keevil
To: George Bowman
Subject: Before and After

George, how was Buddha different before and after his enlightenment? Before Buddha's enlightenment he studied with different teachers and engaged in different practices, looking for an answer to the problems of sickness, old age, and death. After his enlightenment, he had something to share, and traveled all over offering this to many people.

Before Buddha's enlightenment, he was seeking to realize something for himself. After Buddha's enlightenment, he was seeking to share something with others. He realized that the thing he was seeking is already here—he had it, we all have it, completely and fully. With this realization he shifted, from seeking to realize "it," to sharing "it" with others.

Is this how you see it?

From: George Bowman
To: Christopher Keevil
Subject: Before and After

Before, my numberless committee members are endless in variety and difficulty, I vow to save them. After, sentient beings are numberless, I vow to save them.

Is this same or different?

Realization is not something ... it is the absence of something.

*　　*　　*

Me:　　*(Later, during a conversation on the phone)* George, what did you mean by "Before, my numberless committee members are endless in variety and difficulty, I vow to save them ... After, sentient beings are numberless, I vow to save them ... same or different?"

George:　　I thought, if I'm practicing deeply I have many beings that I meet internally. There is the perfectionist. There is the one that feels like a bad dog. There is the one that gets angry when he feels insulted. There are many of them. They are like my internal committee, each with different views and opinions about how I should live my life, what I should do.

When the Buddha is practicing deeply, he is looking into himself and saving himself and many beings there. Then, he is going out into the world to share his insight with others. There are countless beings both inside and outside.

There's an inner process that interacts with the vastness of self-nature, where you stop fighting with yourself. The inner committee members are in service of one another. You find some world of release in your own practice. You see that; then you share it. It's going deeply into yourself, then going out into the marketplace. So, it's not like a break. It's not like—before, you're asleep, and after, you're awake. Rather, it's endless beings inside and outside, with no fixed resting place.

28. When Off the Cushion

Meditation this morning,
silent, still, eyes softly open.
Just This is all there is,
then the idea of "Just This" ... dissipates.

Now very simple:
The feel of legs against the mat,
the windowsill nearby,
a birdsong ripples in the early dawn.

Then,
no dawn,
no windowsill, no legs.
All is calm and bright.

But sadly, this will pass.
What will be there
while dressing for the day
or making breakfast with my wife?

Releasing hope for what will be,
I be with donning pants and shirt
and put an apple slice with almond butter
in my loved one's mouth.

*   *   *

A monk asked Yúnmén, "What is the teaching that transcends
the Buddha and patriarchs?" Yúnmén said, "A sesame bun."

29. Who Saved Who?

I took the spring semester off in my junior year of college. Fully confused about my life's direction, I found myself back at my parent's house with no plans and nothing to do.

My father, in his concern, found me a carpentry job with a middle-aged man named Jonas. Jonas had been out of work when a friend of my father hired him to repair a run-down colonial-era house. Jonas wasn't a carpenter by profession, but he was handy and had done repairs on his own home.

I was also good with my hands, but uninitiated in carpentry. Jonas became my teacher. He showed me how to handle a cat's paw to remove nails, hold a plumb bob to find true vertical, and snap a chalk line—to line things up.

As we worked, we talked. Mostly he talked, and I listened. Not only did I learn about carpentry, I learned how he had lost his family inheritance by trying to build a new tennis center. I learned how he needed willpower to avoid ordering a drink when we went out for lunch together. I learned how he felt when his wife got upset after he left unwashed dishes in the sink. And I heard his heartache when he spoke about his eldest son, who was often wracked by mental illness.

Jonas honored me with his teaching and attention. He wished to be good to everyone and suffered from feelings of falling short.

My time with Jonas changed me. His counsel and care helped me return to college the next semester, and led me to work as a carpenter after college for eight years.

Decades later, I returned to attend Jonas's funeral. He had died of an aneurism. At the service, his four children talked about their father, and how he had told them stories about tunnels under the lawn that led to magical places.

His eldest daughter spoke to me after the service. "You made a great difference to my dad," she said. "That was a difficult time in his life. The way you listened to him when you were working together turned his life around. He was able to get things back together."

*   *   *

A Buddhist teacher said, "When interacting with another person, if you think, 'I am saving you,' there is likely no saving happening."

30. Did I Meet Buddha?

A student asked an eighth-century Zen teacher, "What is Buddha?" The teacher answered, "This very mind is Buddha."

Five centuries later, another Zen teacher wrote a poem commenting on the exchange:

Blue sky and bright sunlight,
No more searching around.
If you ask, "What is Buddha?"

It's like having loot in your pocket and declaring yourself innocent.

I light incense, and sit to meditate, thin smoke rising upward. As I sit, can I know Buddha?

Breath slides into nostrils and rustles out again. "Still the mind." Truck tires whine on the road outside. A crow calls, twice. "Just this. Still the mind."

"I should email Martin. It was so nice seeing him yesterday. But does he still care about me as he used to? We don't get together much anymore."

"Shh … Still the mind."

"I wonder what the title of my book should be? Titles are hard. I'm not good at titles. Writing a book is hard. I've read that even famous authors find writing a book to be hard. Steven King said that …"

"Shh … Still the mind."

It's marvelously quiet. The whole universe centers here. In all directions, horizontal, above and below, no boundary.

"Uh-oh … Hang on! I'll fall off the earth. Just one tilt and I'll fall. Oh crap! Hang on."

"It's OK. Rest in it. It's OK. Rest in the calm."

Rest in the calm.

Calm, vast calm.

Finally, my thinking has stopped.

"No, it hasn't. You just said to yourself, 'My thinking has stopped.'"

"Just let it go. Let it go ..."

Gone.
All gone.
One place.
Only this.
This.
This.

Incense scent is gone.
We must be done.

Oh no,
"Did I meet Buddha?"

*   *   *

A Zen teacher asked his students: "How can you proceed from the top of a hundred-foot pole?"

———
————————
——————
——

31. Who Acts?

One day I drove my son to summer camp in Plymouth, Vermont. After helping him carry his trunk to the cabin and giving a last hug goodbye, I departed around 1:00 in the afternoon, heading toward home. A light drizzle was falling and the road was clear.

As I traveled south on Route 100 along a straight stretch, a large tree ahead on the right started to fall across my path.

Without a moment of thought I swerved sharply to the left across the opposite lane and onto the far shoulder, braking hard. The top of the tree's branches landed heavily across the hood and windshield as the car came to rest on the grass.

Amazingly, the windshield remained intact. Stepping out of the car, I saw several dents in the hood, but otherwise, the car was fine.

I wonder, who was it that swerved the car that day? Who felt the wave of appreciation for being alive?

* * *

George talks about Hua Tou, a form of meditation practice. It consists of holding the question "who?" as the subject of meditation until the practitioner comes to a place of realization before thought.

32. It's Like Light

Properties of light appear nonsensical: light travels past me at the same speed no matter how fast I am moving. It also behaves like a particle *and* a wave, consisting of photons, but making a diffraction pattern when passing through two adjacent narrow slits.

The search for spiritual awakening also appears nonsensical. In eighth-century China, a monk asked a Zen teacher, "Should I try to seek the way?" The teacher replied, "If you try for it, you will become separated from it."

In another story a teacher said, "Do you know, in all the land there is no Zen teacher." A monk responded, "What about those who teach disciples and preside over the assemblies?" The teacher said, "I do not say that there is no Zen, but that there is no Zen teacher."

Adding to the conundrums, Buddha, upon his moment of awakening said, "I and all beings are simultaneously enlightened."

If I seek spiritual realization, I become separated from it. There are no teachers to be found and enlightenment happens to everyone at once. How can I attain it?

There is solace in the properties of light. Something incomprehensible can still be utterly true.

33. Walking through the Chapel Square Mall

There were times when everything became clear.

Like walking through the Chapel Square Mall
shortly before it was decommissioned:
the floor wax yellowing,
the dirty paint peeling,
the dust balls lying in the corners.
Then, riding up the escalator—awestruck—
as the shop-window lights were rubies and opals,
the five-story ceiling an open firmament,
and the shoppers were exactly who they were.

Or, the time with my brother-in-law
when we went out to the side lawn
at the retreat center where he lived,
and we sat cross-legged on the grass,
facing the fields falling away from us
to the ridge on the far side of the valley.
We chanted sutras, and the sky
peeled open and was talking to us,
and the ridge danced and nodded with our song.

And, years ago, in a sunlight-strewn woodland,
strolling on a trail in the mid-afternoon,
down the way a brown bird with red markings
flew off a branch and into the sky,
warbling once as it went.
And at that moment, the lid came off.
The bird, the branch, and every leaf were shimmering
with their own truth,
and all was alright, and just so.

I am buoyed by each of these memories.
But what about now?

*   *   *

Once I asked a friend if he had ever experienced enlightenment. He told me that earlier in his life he had been unreasonably afraid of cars rushing past him when walking along the side of the road. One day when he was out for a walk a car had noisily rushed past him, and suddenly he had felt a vast opening. All his fear dissipated, and he was infused with a profound sense of peace that lasted continuously for several weeks.

34. Ripples of War

Over the years, I have made pilgrimages to the Peace Pagoda in Leverett, Massachusetts. It stands atop a wooded hill; a massive dome painted brilliant white, over one-hundred feet tall.

Constructed in 1985 by a Buddhist monk from Japan along with local volunteers, the pagoda is one of many built by the Nipponzan-Myōhōji monastic order. The order's founder, Nichidatsu Fujii resolved to build pagodas around the world in response to the bombing of Hiroshima and Nagasaki, and for the suffering of innocent people killed and harmed by war.

I took a trip there on a cold February day in 1991. I was troubled by news of war in Iraq, in which the United States was playing a lead role. On the way, I drove through Amherst, a nearby college town. People were standing around a dark pile of something on the ground, and a police officer was there. Wondering about the scene, I continued on.

Arriving at the Peace Pagoda I circumambulated the huge dome three times, slowly and silently. I then walked over to the residence hall where the head nun met me at the front door. "Greetings," she said. "What brings you here?" "This place means a lot to me," I said. "Thank you for making it possible."

The nun heard a phone ring, and stepped inside to take the call. She returned a few minutes later with a look of concern. "A man has immolated himself on the Amherst green," she said, "in protest of the war in Iraq." We stood awhile in silence.

I learned later from the local newspaper that the man, Gregory Levey, had walked onto the Amherst town common with a cardboard sign saying, "Stop the killing." He had stuffed his pants and shirt with newspapers, doused himself with paint thinner, lit a match, and had perished in the flames.

That evening as I drove away from the Peace Pagoda, I stopped in the center of Amherst. A large circle of people stood holding hands in silence on the green. Flowers lay at the location of Mr. Levey's death.

The local paper quoted a college student: "This was more than just a rash act of someone on the edge. It was a moral outcry." Another student said, "This man said war was wrong, and made the ultimate sacrifice."

A Vietnam war veteran was also there, and said, "To have a sign that says stop the killing and then go kill yourself doesn't make a lot of sense, does it?"

The power of that time lives in my heart, and Gregory Levey still calls me to live a life that matters.

*   *   *

On June 11, 1963, at a busy intersection in Saigon, Thích Quảng

Đức, a Vietnamese Buddhist monk, protested injustices of the South Vietnamese government during the Vietnam War by burning himself to death. I was nine years old at the time. The picture of Thích Quảng Đức's self-immolation was published widely around the world. I remember that picture: the seated monk, the flames, and a hundred monks with palms together, witnessing.

---

35. Three Foundations

"Great faith, great doubt, and great courage are the three foundations of practice," says George, quoting from the Zen tradition.

Faith returns me to the practice again and again. Something beckons in the stories of other seekers. The genuine way of those I sit with gives me faith.

Doubt rips and scatters me. Are Zen teachers mostly motivated by ego gratification? Is this silent sitting pointless? Doubt spurs my seeking and drives me to investigate further.

As realization deepens, my preciously held sense of self is laid bare. Nothing is quite as I'd hoped. Each thing I encounter is vividly real. I can no longer imagine that my life is better (or worse) than it actually is. Walking this path takes great courage.

Faith, doubt, and courage—the three foundations of practice.

*　　*　　*

One morning I was sitting with a group of Zen students on retreat at Vallecitos Mountain Retreat Center in New Mexico. The Center lies in a high open valley within the Carson National Forest, at the end of a long dirt road.

George had just finished speaking about great faith, great doubt, and great courage. We were in deep silence. The windows were open and crickets were chirping softly in the fields.

Then, a far-off rumble turned into a horrendous roar as a fighter jet flying low on a training mission came streaking up the valley and over our heads.

In the midst of it we sat ... great faith, great doubt, great courage.

---

36. Upright in the Experience

Me: George, what can I do when I'm suffering emotionally? Some of my most painful moments are when someone gets upset with me, like when a client is disappointed with my work, or when a friend feels I have let them down.

George: Well, you're not alone. I hate disapproval, particularly from someone whose opinion matters to me. It can be very hard. I start to shrink-wrap inside myself ... I may try to be cool, but I'm really not.

Me: But what can I do with the pain? At times it can be really intense.

George: Well, for me, sometimes it's too much, and I need to change my situation. Then I go to the gym, or talk with friends.

Yet at other times I'm able to go into it. Say I'm sitting in *sesshin*; I may feel it is totally beyond me, it's unworkable. Yet if I can become one with the problem — no gap — I don't like it, and it's very uncomfortable ... but when I go there I find enormous brilliance and love.

Me: Say more.

George: People may think that staying upright in their experience means everything will feel fine, but in my experience, it's not like that. It's much more about being present with what is, whatever arises. And sometimes what arises can feel really bad.

In that broken place, we each feel that this makes us untouchable, bad, wrong. And my mind, my ego's defense, will tell me that no one else spends time in this pain. But it's not true. We all circumambulate this *stupa*. So lean into it, try to meet it where it's at.

It requires being willing to give up our curative fantasy of life — that somehow everything will be cured because of enlightenment — and to be emotionally honest about our own life and our reactivity to it.

The question then is how to grow in confidence that the aliveness of this moment is your life, is Buddha's life. The conditions for the occasion of awakening are the contents of your life in this very moment.

37. Wilderness Solo

In my senior year of high school, I took a wilderness survival course. It was held one day a week in the woods behind our school. We learned to fashion a lean-to from branches, start a fire without a match, and make pine-needle tea. The class included twelve students, most in their senior year.

One boy, Harry Snead, had a nasal voice, glasses, and pimples. The boys would joke that he looked like a freak, and the girls would say how they pitied him. Moreover, he didn't seem particularly good at anything. In our high school view of the world, he was just a loser.

Harry would hang at the back of our class, not saying much, as our instructor showed us edible lichens, where to find kindling, and how to keep our clothing dry.

After ten weeks of class it was time for our "solo." We were to spend an overnight alone in the wilderness, using our survival skills. Each person would be at a separate location along a remote trail in the New Hampshire woods. Traveling by school bus, we departed on a Saturday afternoon in May and arrived several hours later at the trailhead. The sky was gray and the air warm and muggy.

Our instructor led us out single file, stopping at intervals to direct each person to their assigned spot. My location was amid young white pines growing under a deciduous canopy. The ground was dotted with groups of ferns. Upon arriving, I set about building a lean-to from pine boughs and fern fronds.

It was not long before the black flies found me. Black flies are small, each one the size of a cracked peppercorn, and they have a nasty, itchy bite. They bit my ears and the back of my neck— over and over again. No amount of swatting would keep them away. After a few hours of this, my ears and neck were hot and swollen from their itchy venom.

As the evening darkness arrived, I felt grateful relief as the black flies departed ... only to have them replaced by little whining mosquitoes. Lying in my lean-to, I could feel them piercing the thin blue jeans I was wearing. I had no protection. Holding back a growing panic, I slept fitfully, gaining some respite from the mosquitoes when it started to rain around 3:00 a.m. The rain dripped on me through the lean-to covering. For the rest of the night I lay in absolute darkness, wet and bitten, waiting for the dawn.

As the first gray light made the trees visible, I stumbled to the trail and headed back to the parking lot where I knew our teacher and a parent chaperone had spent the night with the school bus. I felt such a sense of failure. The solo was a 24-hour event, and we were not supposed to come out of the woods until noon. But I was finished. I couldn't take any more.

When I got back to the bus, I found nearly everyone from the class there. A few people had walked in just as dawn was breaking, like me. But others had come in the prior evening and had slept in the bus, lying on the seats. As I sat in the bus listening to wisecracks about our experience, the last few students straggled in.

The teacher did a roll call, and we suddenly realized that Harry wasn't back. We wondered what had happened. The teacher, looking concerned, went out to find him. When the teacher got to Harry's solo site, he found Harry there, sitting by a fire he had going.

Harry was surprised to see the teacher. At first, he refused to come in, saying he wasn't due until noon. He wanted to complete the solo. But after the teacher told him that everyone else was already back at the bus waiting, he relented.

As Harry climbed on to the bus, everyone grew quiet. "Nice job, Harry," said one person. "Way to go," said another. Harry smiled quietly and went to take his seat.

38. She Was Just Here

A feeling, acrid and sharp, rises from my solar plexus
as the memory comes again
of our dear friend Laurissa,
who passed away from cancer this Saturday morning.

We drove to her house the day after she died there,
and sat with a few friends in her backyard
around a low fire, burning sprigs of sage.
"She was so engaged and welcoming when we saw her last,"
said my wife, "and that was just a week ago."

I am dumbfounded.
How can it be that
she will no longer pick up the phone
or offer a heartfelt embrace?

There are Zen teachings of "the unborn" in each of us,
and when chanting the *Heart Sutra* we say,
"No old age and death, and also no extinction of it."
Yet these offer little solace now; my grief remains.

Settling into
the vast uncharted territory of unknowing,
I begin to see, like the sun becoming just visible
through early morning fog,

that the sorrow of death
accompanies every moment of every day—as thoughts
dissipate, conversations falter,
or visits come to an end.

At the same time,
a joy of being alive
is interlaced with it all.
And everything that arises,
every thought, object, person, or event,
transmutes and emerges from what is already here.

Comes death, then life.
No death. No life.
Only death. Only life.
This death. This life.

*   *   *

Buddha said, "Of all the footprints, that of the elephant is supreme. Of all meditations, that on death is supreme."

Meditation on one's own death, also called *maraṇasati* meditation, is one of the oldest practices in the Buddhist tradition. The practice is a series of visualizations of one's body after death going through the sequence of decay: decomposing flesh, then a bare skeleton, and finally only dust.

39. Fraction Over Infinity-Zero

Zen Teacher Yamada Koun said, all phenomena is a fraction over infinity-zero. Like this:

$$\frac{\alpha}{\infty}$$

The numerator is the particular expression and the denominator is pure principle.

It's the interplay of relative and absolute: I enact my life with its specifics, yet all the while there is the timeless and eternal.

The cat, lying on my desk as I write, with pink ears and soft, white fur, purrs in quiet contentment, his eyes closed.

The phone line workers outside my window, muscular and yellow-vested, with their bucket truck, deftly plant a new pole and re-attach power lines downed by a tree limb earlier today.

As I water the houseplants, our geranium offers its peculiar smell, which carries an early memory of my mother holding me and tending the geranium in our kitchen.

And sitting again at my desk, my breathing rises and falls of its own accord as I concentrate, finishing the words on this page.

Each moment—a fraction over infinity-zero. The relative, and the absolute.

But which part is the relative, and which part the absolute?

40. Mowing Lawns

Jack Durham was a friend of mine in high school. Together we had a summer lawn-mowing business. Dressed in denim overalls and tee shirts, we would load our two mowers into my mother's Volkswagen bus with the middle seats removed and travel to lawns around town. We had a two-gallon gas can for the mowers and a cooler of iced tea for us.

One of our lawn mowers had a Briggs & Stratton engine that always worked. The other mower had a Tecumseh engine. I would clean the spark plug, flush the air filter, check the flywheel cotter pin, but still it had trouble starting. We would agree it was badly made, and stupid. My tools would come out again.

At lunchtime, Jack would tell me about the time with his girlfriend the night before. I would share my mother's chocolate chip cookies. We would say they were the absolute best. Jack would come up with ideas for the weekend—like an open-air folk dance gathering we attended with our girlfriends at Copley Square with hundreds of people, all smiling.

Jack and I talked about parents, professions, and what made a meaningful life. He was the best friend I had known.

"Jack," I said, one day, "How is it that you always do a little more for me than I do for you?" "Really?" he said, surprised. "It's you who always does a little more for me."

41. Pushing the Pendulum

As a boy, I loved going to the Museum of Science in Boston. There was a massive pendulum in the front lobby, its cable five stories high. The pendulum's huge brass orb would greet us on arrival, swinging slowly and gracefully across a 12-point design on the floor.

A sign explained that this type of pendulum was invented by a French physicist named Léon Foucault, to demonstrate the rotation of the earth.

Along the edge of the swing path small domino-like objects were placed at equal intervals. Every ten minutes the pendulum's tip, swinging close to the ground, would intersect with a domino and tip it over. By watching the dominoes fall, it was clear that the pendulum was slowly rotating in its path, its axis shifting direction over time. Actually, the pendulum's axis stayed the same, while the earth rotated under it, making the pendulum knock over the dominoes.

To keep the pendulum going, a museum employee would occasionally crouch at the end of the pendulum's swing path, and with a soft white cloth give the pendulum a gentle push.

The whole arrangement made mysterious forces visible— the pendulum's swing, the falling dominoes, the rotation of the earth. The employee appeared as a minor factor, contributing an occasional push to maintain momentum.

It seems my own life is like that: inexorable swings of emotion, knocked-over expectations, and the slow rotation of growth and aging. The best I can do is give a little push.

42. An Apology

In my days as a professional carpenter, I had a boss named Gordon. He was strong and lithe, an architect by training, and a builder of solar homes. He designed the homes he built, hiring a crew of four and working as the lead with a hammer and nail apron.

Gordon was fast, incredibly fast. Once, working alone, he built a dormer in two days—studs, sheetrock, window, and roofing—the whole thing. He could get us to frame a house faster than anyone else I knew.

His knack was seeing many steps ahead, and knowing how all the pieces would come together. At a job site on his crew, we would move in a coordinated dance, with little waste of time or action. I learned speed and efficiency, and how to sustain it throughout the day.

But Gordon's speed was hard to take. Many days I felt rushed and pushed. As the months went by, an anger grew in my chest, but I hesitated to say anything. He was my boss.

One morning on the job, we were assembling forms for a foundation. We placed vertical plywood sheets connected by steel tie rods in a dirt trench to form the shape into which the cement truck would pour. And the cement truck was coming. The arrival time was 10:00 a.m. and we had to get everything in place by then. The truck had to pour as soon as it arrived or the concrete would harden in its belly.

We were behind schedule, and Gordon was pushing. Racing around and barking orders, he drove us faster and faster. Tensions rose. Finally, I'd had enough. The cork popped off. "Slow down," I screamed. "You're driving us crazy." He looked at me with open eyes, and stopped.

"I'm sorry," he said. "I'm sorry." I could tell he had really heard me. All of a sudden, I felt his care for me, a genuine, personal care. I could also feel the urgency of the situation in a new way. "Come on," I said, "Let's keep going." We finished the forms just as the concrete truck drove up.

After work that day, we sat a while and talked. I told him how angry I had become with him because he was always pushing. He talked about the challenges of house building, and the responsibility he carried to get things right.

His apology melted something in me. Before, I had thought that Gordon had to change for me to accept him. But after that day I saw him differently. I could see the pressure he was under. He still pushed hard and was incredibly fast, but I could tell him to calm down when it became too much, and he would listen.

We remained friends for years after I moved away. And I never forgot what I learned about working fast, or the power of an honest apology.

---

43. Anybody In?

A Zen teacher asked the hermit, "Anybody in?"

Today, I ask myself: Anybody in?

When am I in?
When am I not in?

Always in.

Sometimes thinking I'm in when I'm not.

Sometimes thinking I'm not in when I am.

Sometimes not thinking.

---

44. Actually, Not a Problem

George lives in a log cabin at Furnace Mountain Zen Center in Kentucky. It's a modest yet lovely dwelling. There is a sleeping loft overhead, a cozy kitchen, a wood stove, spiritual books on the shelves, and a buddha on the altar. The walls are made of trees felled from the property. Outside against the back wall is a little shed for the water heater.

At Furnace Mountain there are many structures—sleeping cabins, a teahouse, and the blue-roofed temple where retreats are held. The buildings rest among stands of oak and hickory and are joined by gravel paths.

Furnace Mountain also has pack rats. They can grow to be a foot long and love chewing the innards of walls and structures. The damage can be a problem, and the monks and nuns do their best to keep them out.

One day while George was away, a pack rat chewed the electrical wiring running into the water heater. The chewing made sparks and the sparks started a fire. The fire threatened to burn the cabin down. As the fire grew, it melted a plastic water pipe above the heater. The water sprayed the fire. The fire went out.

Upon returning home, George smelled something. Checking

behind his cabin, he saw what had happened.

Only a bit of clean-up was required.

*   *   *

Zen Master Mǎzǔ *was* seriously ill. The temple superintendent asked him, "Teacher, how are you feeling these days?" Master Mǎzǔ replied, "Sun-face Buddha, Moon-face Buddha."

---

45. Either Or

A poem by a sixth-century Zen teacher, called *Faith in Mind*, opens with the following:

> *The Great Way is not difficult*
> *Only avoid picking and choosing.*
> *If you don't grasp or reject,*
> *It fully reveals itself.*

I used to work for a large advisory firm where corporations hired us to solve business problems, such as how to increase the speed of developing new telephone cable connectors, or how to produce orange juice at lower cost.

In trying to solve a problem, it would often seem like solutions were hampered by an "either-or." Faster development of telephone cable connectors would lead to higher failure rates. Lower cost in producing orange juice would compromise the taste.

Our telephone-cable client was turning out new types of cable connectors in nine months. The new-product design team was convinced if the time was shortened, failure rates would rise. But we started calling around and found a Japanese company that was turning out new products with excellent quality in two-and-a-half months.

The design team was stunned. But when together we looked carefully at the design process, unnecessary steps and redundancies revealed themselves. As a result, our client was able to develop new products at the same quality in three months thereby getting to market faster. Sales volumes rose. The team was elated.

Our orange juice client wanted to reduce unit cost. But much of the cost was in the oranges coming from the growers. This cost was tied to quality. "Good-tasting orange juice requires tasty oranges," said Walter, the head of manufacturing. "And these oranges are priced by the market. You can't reduce this cost without compromising the product," he said adamantly.

One day Walter and I were walking through the plant. We watched the orange trucks arriving, stopping on the scales at the entry point. A sample of fruit was taken from each truck to ensure overall quality. The grower would be paid for the weight of oranges in the truck.

After being unloaded, the oranges were carried by conveyor belt through the culling station. Bad oranges were removed, leaving good oranges to enter the juicer.

Suddenly Walter exclaimed, "Why not track the culled fruit back to each truck, and only pay the grower for the good oranges?"

The orange juice plant started doing this, which caused the growers to become more selective with what they put on their trucks. As a result, unit cost went down, throughput increased, and quality stayed high. Walter was delighted.

In each case our client moved beyond an apparent either-or. A solution previously unseen revealed itself.

*   *   *

In the time of Buddha, two companions were on a journey. Their path went through a thick forest. In the darkest part of the forest, a criminal stepped out from behind a tree wielding a large knife. "One of you is going to die," he said, "the other I will let go." If you were one of those two companions, what would you do?

_____

_____

___

46. Compassion

Me: George, my mother recently asked if Zen teaches compassion. In our conversations about Zen, she says that compassion hasn't come up very much. What are your thoughts? Does Zen teach compassion?

George: As I see it, the whole teaching is about understanding and compassion. It's about taming one's mind and that leads to intensifying one's compassion for the world.

In truly seeing your own pain, you see this is the way of the world; we're all in deep shit. There is suffering, and there is a way of working with this suffering.

My teacher Soen Sa Nim used to say, to make a point, "*Samadhi* is a drug. What really matters is your wish to be of service in the world. I don't care if you're enlightened. I just care if you're helpful."

I have a great incentive to tame my mind, not just for myself, but because I talk to you. I look at my own reactivity, doubts, and confusion, yet I'm inspired to use them in some way because I talk to you. If I didn't talk to you, there'd be no edge. And, it's the same for you with all of your clients, all these people who mean well. Their primary problem is others, and themselves. You have the incentive to tame your doubts and reactivity because of them.

*   *   *

Recently while on retreat I was bowing 108 times to Avalokitesvara, the bodhisattva who hears the cries of the world. It was before dawn and others had not yet arrived in the meditation hall. Following the traditional practice of bowing, I stood erect, palms together, then lifted my joined palms above my head. I then placed palms on the floor, kneeled, touched my forehead to the floor, and raised my palms upward past my ears. Then I returned to standing, palms together.

As I did this repeatedly, everything began to drop away. The stillness, the offering of my self and body were all there was. Tears of recognition began to wash my face — for my own failings, my loved-ones' yearnings, my clients' fears, the ineptitudes of our political leaders. We are all struggling … and all blessed.

47. Leader of the Choir

John Worthington conducted my high school choir. His passion for music carried us on its wings. We sang for our peers at school assemblies. We sang for our parents at evening concerts. We went on tour to sing for other schools. And we performed with the Boston Symphony Orchestra at Symphony Hall.

On stage, we were one voice. Our sound was wistful and pensive as we sang Robert Frost's *Road Not Taken*, a poem about choosing one's path in life. At our high school's annual homecoming concert, alumni would join us for Handel's *Hallelujah Chorus*. My scalp would tingle and a smile would burst forth as we moved up the crescendos in that piece.

Mr. Worthington helped us to sing better than we ever imagined we could. And his care for each of us fostered our care for each other. I caught the flu on tour one year and was laid up in bed all alone for a day at a host family's house. Unannounced, six of my fellow choir members came over to cheer me up.

Mr. Worthington was also a guidance counselor. I dropped by his office regularly in my senior year, wondering which college I should apply to, or what my life goals should be. He would listen, his gaze penetrating and attentive. Leaving his office, I would feel courage. I had something to offer after all.

Even as Mr. Worthington lifted us, he faced his own demons. He smoked heavily, and told us he should quit, but never did. He went through a divorce, after which his brow was more furrowed and his eyes more distracted. And he became increasingly deaf, cocking his head and asking us to repeat things. I saw him some years after graduation and he grimaced, saying that he could no longer hear the choir and had taken a job selling hearing aids.

When he passed away—from lung cancer—a church service was held in town. In was filled to overflowing.

48. Coming Home

In the end, somehow,
everything is OK.

Together we have come
exactly this far.

The answer
emerges as the searching.

Suffering a loss
is suffering of loss.

Arriving here again
for the first time.

Many events and cognitions;
one true life.

If it seems my self ends when this body ends,
that's an imagination.

All beings, and all time
is just here ... and now.

*　　*　　*

That may be so, but what should we have for dinner given the refrigerator's been broken for the whole time we've been gone?

Additional Resources

Bo Mun's Ten Principles of Zen[1]

Me: George, as I reflect over our years of interactions, I realize there is a set of themes that keep coming up.

George: Yes, there is a set of fundamentals in this work, a set of principles. There aren't very many of them, I'd say about ten.

Me: Now I'm curious. Can you say what they are?

George: Yes, let me see:

(1) First, there's the fundamental point of *pure possibility*. This is the *Dharmakāya*,[2] the foundation of the mind that doesn't know, and can meet anything, do anything. This is stopping, sitting on the cushion. It is the foundation.

(2) If that is experienced, if the foundation is somewhat clear, then there is the possibility *to appreciate* what comes in front of the mirror of the self. This is the *Saṃbhogakāya*,[3] the bliss body, the body of appreciation, where you have the capacity to appreciate anything. It's sitting upright in the midst of it all, and cutting the gap between the observer and the observed. It's true love and understanding. It's where self meets self.

(3) And, in the appreciation, inevitably there is the *call to action*. This is the *Nirmāṇakāya*,[4] the body of function. Something is required. The bird sings. The dog barks. We return to this over and over. When you're called forth to action, you fully engage body and mind. You do carpentry. You give the talk. This is to forget the self in the activity of doing something. This is the work of "function," calling yourself forward in service of what you know to be most true.

    Each of these three (stopping, appreciating, acting) is contained in the other two, and in each one there are worlds within worlds. At whatever place we find ourselves, it's possible to go deeper. That's one of my greatest debts and gratitudes to my teacher Sasaki Roshi. He would push me to go deeper. And in the same way, I want you to recognize your mind, and I push you to go deeper.

(4) Then in this study of Zen we engage in, there is the Big Self as possibility, and the particular expression of the self, which is the immediacy of one's life. The way you can enter into this is by *not knowing*. This not knowing is touching and being touched by God. It's to see "it" clearly, experientially, and to personify it, bringing it more and more into your life.

(5) Then, there is the interplay of *the relative and the absolute*, which is described in many ways in the Zen tradition, such as in the four manifestations of host and guest in the Rinzai tradition, or Tozan's Five Ranks in the Soto tradition. We grow in our ability to exchange self for other. These are, of course, all just a way of talking, or of singing a love song.

(6) There is the principle of the secret, or *the emotional imperative*. The secret is that the greatest power and strength will be found where you most don't want to go. Embedded in every relationship is this sense of the imperative, the assumptions that are your deepest conditioning, that you'd never want to let go of. The willingness to enter into the imperative is the foundation of self-study. This is the *shigyo* practice, the dying practice. It is the fight between husband and wife, the frozen-ness, the fixation, the impulse of necessity: "I must do this or I can't live without her." And, there's a fundamental rebirth if you truly enter into it.

(7) All of this requires *great faith, great doubt, and great courage*. These spur us on in our practice. That's so core.

(8) There is the principle of *no fixed position*. Nothing remains as it is. Everything keeps shape-shifting. This principle is combined with all the other principles.

(9) And, there is *cycling through it all*. We go round and round. "I thought I was done with falling in love, and now I'm

smitten all over again. What am I going to do?" Soen Sa Nim[5] would talk about the zero-degree point and the three-hundred-and-sixty- degree point on the circle. They are the same. Our practice is about returning to the same spot with no opinion. But it's actually like an alpha helix. I return to the same place, but it's been refreshed. I meet the same places, I've been here a million times, and I've never been here before.

(10) Finally, *we can't do this alone*. When I was young, I used to do a lot of meditation practice on my own. But I found it's the sangha that helps us through. We're all in this together—it's a deep democracy.

*   *   *

1   George Bowman's dharma name as a Zen Master is "Bo Mun," meaning "Wide Gate."

2   The term *Dharmakāya* refers to the "absolute," or "truth body," representing the transcendence of form of the five senses—and realization of true thusness.

3   *Saṃbhogakāya* means "the body of mutual enjoyment," "bliss body," or "clear-light manifestation."

4   The *Nirmāṇakāya*, or "created body" manifests in time and space.

5   The honorific title for George's teacher Seung Sahn.

The 48 pieces in this book each depict one or more of Bomun's Ten Principles of Zen, as shown in the table below.

Pieces	The principles they illustrate
1. 4:30 a.m.	*(1) Pure possibility*
2. In the Subway	*(3) The call to action*
	(10) We can't do this alone
3. When the Engine Stops	*(3) The call to action*
4. I Choose This	*(2) To appreciate*
5. Red Geranium	*(2) To appreciate*
6. When the Door Opened	*(6) The emotional imperative*
	(10) We can't do this alone
7. Why Do You Meditate?	*(2) To appreciate*
	(3) The call to action
	(7) Great faith, great doubt, great courage
8. Today	*(3) The call to action*
9. Distant Temple Bell	*(1) Pure possibility*
	(2) To appreciate
10. Going to the Still Center	*(6) The emotional imperative*
11. The Winner and the Loser	
	(8) No fixed position

Pieces	The principles they illustrate
12. Is It Possible?	*(6) The emotional imperative* *(8) No fixed position* *(9) Cycling through it all*
13. Buddha, the Window Washer	*(3) The call to action*
14. Who Is This Someone?	*(2) To appreciate* *(3) The call to action*
15. Jock Strap	*(3) The call to action*
16. When Will It Come?	*(4) Not knowing*
17. Hotel Room	*(1) Pure possibility*
18. Stages or No Stages?	*(3) The call to action* *(4) Not knowing* *(9) Cycling through it all*
19. Why Not? Because He Didn't	*(6) The emotional imperative* *(9) Cycling through it all*
20. The Question	*(4) Not knowing* *(7) Great faith, great doubt, great courage* *(9) Cycling through it all*
21. A Place to Stay	*(6) The emotional imperative* *(10) We can't do this alone*

Pieces	The principles they illustrate
22. On Retreat	(1) *Pure possibility* (2) *To appreciate*
23. I Didn't Think It Would Be Like This	(6) *The emotional imperative*
24. Ordinary Mind	(2) *To appreciate* (3) *The call to action*
25. Stop!	(1) *Pure possibility* (4) *Not knowing*
26. Kindness	(6) *The emotional imperative* (10) *We can't do this alone*
27. Before and After	(8) *No fixed position*
28. When Off the Cushion	(2) *To appreciate* (3) *The call to action*
29. Who Saved Who?	(8) *No fixed position* (10) *We can't do it alone*
30. Did I Meet Buddha?	(1) *Pure possibility* (3) *The call to action* (7) *Great faith, great doubt, great courage*
31. Who Acts?	(3) *The call to action*
32. It's Like Light	(4) *Not knowing*

Pieces	The principles they illustrate
33. Walking Through the Chapel Square Mall	*(2) To appreciate*
34. Ripples of War	*(10) We can't do it alone*
35. Three Foundations	*(7) Great faith, great doubt, great courage*
36. Upright in the Experience	*(6) The emotional imperative*
37. Wilderness Solo	*(8) No fixed position*
38. She Was Just Here	*(8) No fixed position*
39. Fraction over Infinity-Zero	*(5) The relative and the absolute*
40. Mowing Lawns	*(5) The relative and the absolute* *(10) We can't do this alone*
41. Pushing the Pendulum	*(2) To appreciate* *(8) No fixed position*
42. An Apology	*(10) We can't do this alone*
43. Anybody In?	*(1) Pure possibility* *(7) Great faith, great doubt, great courage*
44. Actually, Not a Problem	*(8) No fixed position*

Pieces	The principles they illustrate
45. Either Or	*(4) Not knowing*
46. Compassion	*(2) To appreciate* *(10) We can't do this alone*
47. Leader of the Choir	*(8) No fixed position* *(10) We can't do this alone*
48. Coming Home	*(1–10) All ten principles*

Bomun's Ten Principles of Zen are each illustrated by multiple pieces in the book, as shown in the table below.

The ten principles	Pieces that illustrate them
(1) Pure possibility	1. 4:30 a.m. 9. Distant Temple Bell 17. Hotel Room 22. On Retreat 25. Stop! 30. Did I Meet Buddha? 43. Anybody In? 48. Coming Home
(2) To appreciate	4. I Choose This 5. Red Geranium 7. Today 9. Distant Temple Bell 14. Who Is This Someone? 22. On Retreat 24. Ordinary Mind 28. When Off the Cushion

The ten principles	Pieces that illustrate them
	33. Walking Through the Chapel Square Mall
	41. Pushing the Pendulum
	46. Compassion
	48. Coming Home
(3) The call to action	2. In the Subway
	3. When the Engine Stops
	7. Why Do You Meditate?
	8. Today
	13. Buddha, The Window Washer
	14. Who Is This Someone?
	15. Jock Strap
	18. Stages or No Stages?
	24. Ordinary Mind
	28. When Off the Cushion
	30. Did I Meet Buddha?
	31. Who Acts?
	48. Coming Home
(4) Not knowing	16. When Will It Come?
	18. Stages or No Stages?
	20. The Question
	25. Stop!
	32. It's Like Light
	45. Either Or
	48. Coming Home
(5) The relative and the absolute	39. Fraction over Infinity-Zero
	40. Mowing Lawns
	48. Coming Home

The ten principles	**Pieces that illustrate them**
(6) The emotional imperative	6. When the Door Opened
	10. Going to the Still Center
	12. Is It Possible?
	19. Why Not? Because He Didn't
	21. A Place to Stay
	23. I Didn't Think It Would Be Like This
	26. Kindness
	36. Upright in the Experience
	48. Coming Home
(7) Great faith, great doubt, *great courage*	7. Why Do You Meditate?
	20. The Question
	30. Did I Meet Buddha?
	35. Three Foundations
	43. Anybody In?
	48. Coming Home
(8) No fixed position	11. The Winner and the Loser
	12. Is It Possible?
	27. Before and After
	29. Who Saved Who?
	37. Wilderness Solo
	38. She Was Just Here
	41. Pushing the Pendulum
	44. Actually, Not a Problem
	47. Leader of the Choir
	48. Coming Home
(9) Cycling through it all	12. Is It Possible?
	18. Stages or No Stages?
	19. Why Not? Because He Didn't

The ten principles	Pieces that illustrate them
	20. The Question
	48. Coming Home
(10) We can't do this alone	2. In the Subway
	6. When the Door Opened
	21. A Place to Stay
	26. Kindness
	29. Who Saved Who?
	34. Ripples of War
	40. Mowing Lawns
	42. An Apology
	46. Compassion
	47. Leader of the Choir
	48. Coming Home

Endnotes

Foreword

"Dizang asked Fayen, 'Where are you going?'" This exchange is found in *Case 20, Dizang's Nearness,* in the *Book of Serenity,* a collection of 100 koans, or Zen teaching stories written in eleventh-century China by Wànsōng Xíngxiù and published in the thirteenth century by Hóngzhì Zhēngjué.

"The Zen stick ..." Zen Masters typically keep a short stick with them while teaching. In formal Zen settings the stick is symbolic of the Master's authority to teach. In this case George passed his stick around the circle to act as a talking stick.

4. I Choose This

"When hot or cold come, how can I avoid them?" This story is found in Case 43 of *The Blue Cliff Record,* another collection of 100 koans, compiled by Xuedou Chongxian in the eleventh century, and expanded in the twelfth century by Yuanwu Keqin.

5. Red Geranium

"A monk met an old woman ..." This story is found in Case 28 of *The Gateless Gate,* which is a collection of 48 koans compiled in the thirteenth century by the Chinese Zen Master Mumon Ekai.

"... buy refreshments ..." The Chinese character used in the original text for "refreshments" is *tenjin,* which has a double meaning: it can mean a popular confection made from flour, bean paste, and sugar, or it can mean, "to light up the mind."

10. Going to the Still Center

"... I vow with all beings ..." This phrase is commonly used as the second phrase in four-phrase Buddhist gathas used for reflection. It recognizes that we all face elements of challenge, such as anger, as part of our shared condition with all sentient beings.

11. The Winner and the Loser

"The monks at a Zen monastery assemble to listen ..." This story comes from Case 26 of *The Gateless Gate*.

12. Is It Possible?

"... and Dōgen Zenji ..." Dōgen Zenji was the founder of the Sōtō school of Zen and lived in Japan from 1200–1253.

"Life in the form of ..." George uses this phrase referring to the interplay of the relative and the absolute. We each express the absolute essence of life through the relative form and actions we each take.

13. Buddha, the Window Washer

"The most profound love arises ..." This quote comes loosely from the Torei Zenji's bodhisattva vow, which is chanted by Zen groups.

14. Who Is This Someone?

"Even Buddha is a servant of someone else ..." This exchange is found in Case 45 of *The Gateless Gate*.

16. When Will It Come?

"Kyōgen, as a young monk ..." This story can be found in the notes section of Case 5 of *The Gateless Gate*, translated with commentary by Katsuki Sekida. Kyōgen was a monk in ninth-century China.

18. Stages or No Stages?

"*The Flower Ornament Scripture* ..." See chapter 26 of the

Avatamsaka Sutra, or *Flower Ornament Scripture.* The scripture was composed in third-century India.

"... the *Lankavatara Sutra* and the *Surangama Sutra* ..." these are other influential texts in the Zen tradition.

"... the *Ten Ox-herding Pictures* ..." are a series of short poems and accompanying drawings used in the Zen tradition which emerged in twelfth-century China.

"The *Heart Sutra* ..." is chanted by Buddhist groups around the world and is a brief encapsulation of the breadth of Buddhist teachings.

"Dae Gak, who also received transmission from George's teacher ..." Dae Gak (Robert Genthner) leads the Furnace Mountain Zen Retreat Center in Clay City, Kentucky, where George also lives. He gave the talk I refer to in this piece on July 7, 2018, during a retreat at Furnace Mountain.

"Ken Wilbur, a spiritual pundit ..." Ken Wilbur has published many books on Buddhism and spirituality. He refers to himself as a spiritual pundit.

"Charlotte Joko Beck, who was a Zen teacher in Los Angeles ..." Charlotte Joko Beck (1917–2011) studied with Hakuyu Taizan Maezumi, Hakuun Yasutani, and Soen Nakagawa. She was the guiding teacher for Zen Center San Diego and wrote several books on Zen.

"Dogen ... wrote that a person who is enlightened may not know they are enlightened." See the *Genjōkōan* in *Shōbōgenzō*, by Dogen (1200–1253), a Japanese Zen teacher and founder of the Soto Zen School. Also see the quote: "Those who study the way seek to be immersed in the way. For those who are immersed in the way, all traces of enlightenment perish." From *Moon in a Dewdrop: Writings of Zen Master Dōgen*, edited by Kazuaki Tanahashi, New York: North Point Press, 1985, p. 42

"...I and all beings awaken simultaneously." See the story of Buddha's awakening in the first chapter of *Transmission of*

Light: Zen in the Art of Enlightenment by Zen Master Keizan.

19. Why Not? Because He Didn't

"Why did Daitsu Chisho Buddha ..." is found in Case 9 of *The Gateless Gate*.

20. The Question

"The oak tree in the garden." This exchange is found in Case 37 of *The Gateless Gate*. Zen Master Jōshū as he is known in Japan, or Zhàozhōu Cōngshěn, lived in China in the eighth to ninth centuries.

22. On Retreat

The location of the retreat referred to in this piece was at Furnace Mountain Zen Retreat Center in Clay City, Kentucky. "Eyes open, lids soft, gazing forty-five degrees down ..." In Zen, practitioners meditate with their eyes softly open, gazing down at a roughly forth-five-degree angle, not focusing on anything specific.

23. I Didn't Think It Would Be Like This

The tale of the tigers and the delicious strawberry can be found in *Kindness: A Treasury of Buddhist Wisdom for Children and Parents*, collected and adapted by Sarah Conover.

24. Ordinary Mind

"Ordinary mind is the way." This is excerpted from Case 19 in *The Gateless Gate*, which relates an exchange between a Zen student and teacher in ninth-century China. The full exchange proceeds thus: Jōshū asked Nánquán, "What is the Way?" Nánquán replied, "Ordinary mind is the Way." "Shall I seek for it?" Jōshū asked. "If you try for it, you become separated from it," said Nánquán. "How can I know the Way unless I try for it?" responded Jōshū. Nánquán replied, "The Way is not about knowing or not knowing. Knowing is delusion; not knowing is blankness. When you reach the Way beyond doubt, you will find it as vast and boundless as outer space. How can it be discussed on the level of right or wrong?" At these words, Jōshū had a sudden realization.

"This thought comes from Buddha-mind, this thought is one with Buddha-mind" comes from the following Zen chant, repeated ten times with increasing speed to the rhythm of the wood block:

Kanzeon!
Praise to Buddha
All are one with Buddha,
All awake to Buddha.
Buddha, Dharma, Sangha:
Freedom, joy and purity.
Through the day Kanzeon,
Through the night Kanzeon.
This thought comes from Buddha-mind.
This thought is one with Buddha mind.

25. Stop!

On page 69 of *Zen Mind, Beginners Mind* by Shunryu Suzuki, founder of the San Francisco Zen Center, there is nothing but a life-size and lifelike imprint of a house fly.

26. Kindness

Pan Am Flight 103 was traveling from London to New York on December 21, 1988. At 7:01 p.m. the aircraft was destroyed by a bomb, killing all 243 passengers and 16 crew. Large sections of the aircraft fell on to residential areas, killing 11 more people on the ground. On August 16, 2003 Libya formally accepted responsibility for the bombing.

27. Before and After

For a beautiful rendition of Buddha's life and teaching, see *Old Path, White Clouds* by Thich Nhat Hanh.

28. When Off the Cushion

"A sesame bun." This exchange occurs in Case 77 of *The Blue Cliff Record*. It also occurs in Case 78 of the *Book of Serenity*.

30. Did I Meet Buddha?

"An eighth-century Zen teacher was asked by a student, 'What is Buddha?'" and, "Blue sky and bright sunlight …" This exchange and poem are Case 30 of *The Gateless Gate*.

"… having loot in your pocket and declaring yourself innocent." A story with similarities to this phrase is found in the *Lotus Sutra*, in the parable of The Jewel Hidden in the Robe.

Once there was a man who had a rich friend. One evening the man called upon his friend, who entertained him with a delicious meal and fine wine. Following the meal, the man fell fast asleep, and could not be aroused.

The rich friend had to depart that night on a long business trip. He had hoped to give the man a gift, a gem of great worth, before leaving. Given that the man was fast asleep, the friend sewed the gem into the hem of the sleeping man's robe.

The man awoke the next morning finding his friend gone, unaware of the gem in his robe. Not long after, the man sank into poverty and wandered here and there, facing untold hardships. After many years, he unexpectedly ran into his old friend.

The man's friend, surprised by the man's condition, told him about the gem, which had always been with him.

"… proceed from the top of a 100-foot pole." This question is found in Case 46 of *The Gateless Gate*.

32. Who Acts?

"George talks about Hua Tou ..." Hua Tou practice is a form of meditation found in Korean, Chinese and Japanese (Rinzai) Zen. To practice Hua Tou, one concentrates on a phrase, initially repeating it silently with a questioning and open mind and then thinking about "Who" or "What" is generating the Hua Tou. The practice was introduced by the Chinese Zen master Dahui Zonggao in the twelfth century, who emphasized it for lay people. It is described in the book *Tracing Back the Radiance: Chinul's Korean Way to Zen*.

32. It's Like Light

"If you try for it, you will become separated from it." This comes from Case 19 of *The Gateless Gate*, as cited above.
"... there is no Zen teacher." This exchange is found in Case 11 of *The Blue Cliff Record*.
"I and all beings are simultaneously enlightened." See Case 1 of *Transmission of Light*, a set of enlightenment stories for successive Buddhist teachers beginning with Buddha.

35. Three Foundations

"Great Faith, great doubt, and great courage are the three foundations of practice." George uses this phrase, as do others in the Korean Zen tradition. Hakuin (1686–1768), a Japanese Zen Master also used this phrase, often translated as "great faith, great doubt, great determination."

36. Upright in the Experience

"... sitting in *sesshin* ..." *Sesshin* is a Japanese word referring to an intensive period of Zen meditation in a monastery or retreat center.
"... stupa ..." A *stupa* is a commemorative Buddhist monument. Meditators will circumambulate a stupa (walk slowly around it multiple times) as a meditation practice.

38. She Was Just Here

"Of all the footprints..." is found in the *Mahaparinirvana Sutta*, chapter 3.

39. Fraction Over Infinity-Zero

Yamada Kōun, (1907–1989) was a Japanese Zen teacher who deemphasized the separation between laypeople and the ordained.

43. Anybody in?

"A Zen teacher came to the hermit's cottage and asked, 'Anybody in?'" This question begins Case 11 of *The Gateless Gate*.

44. Actually, Not a Problem

"... Zen Master Mazu ..." This exchange is found in Case 3 of the *Blue Cliff Record*. Mǎzǔ Dàoyī lived in eighth-century China.

45. Either Or

"The Great Way is not difficult ..." is a poem that has been traditionally attributed to Zen Master Jiànzhì Sēngcàn (died 606). However, scholars now generally believe that the verse was written well after Sēngcàn's death, probably during the Tang Dynasty (618–907).

"If you were one of those two companions, what would you do?" At first, one might feel like saying, "Kill the other person." Or wanting to be selfless, one might imagine offering one's own life. But there are many possible responses that go beyond the apparent either-or of the situation.

46. Compassion

"... samadhi ..." is a state of deep meditative absorption.

48. Coming Home

"... given the refrigerator's been broken ..." this phrase recalls when my wife and I had been away for the summer and arrived home thinking about dinner. We opened the freezer door and were hit by the stench of rotting salmon. We had purchased a case of fresh salmon, but the refrigerator had been off while we were away.

Acknowledgments

My great appreciation goes to George Bowman who has contributed so much to my love of Zen, along with his two main teachers, Seung Sahn, who first brought Zen to Providence, Rhode Island, from Korea, and Kyozan Jōshū Sasaki, who came from Japan to California and inspired a whole generation of practitioners. Thank you also to several of George's long-time students who gave me feedback and suggestions: John Wark, an author and editor who provided guidance and encouragement on tone, titling, and the order of pieces; Jian (David Klinger), who reflected so thoughtfully on the text; and Gary Beard who caringly reviewed the writing.

I also appreciate friends who not only provided editorial suggestions but have inspired me in Buddhist meditation practice: Paul Bloom, a guiding teacher at the New Haven Zen Center, and Beth Roth, who teaches, practices, and writes about mindfulness meditation. Anne Dutton, leader of the East Rock Sangha, also brought her truth-informed eye to the writing.

Members of my family gave editorial help: my mother, Hannah Keevil, who read and commented on four different drafts; my older brother, Terry Keevil, who has been a guiding light in my life and responded to the writing with honesty and authenticity; Marlowe Miller, a professor of English who gave me feedback in the most supportive way; my brother-in-law John de Kadt, a poet and internationally-known drummer for Kirtan music; and Kai Keevil, my son, who offered useful and insightful suggestions for the text.

Dear friends have also been helpful, including Dick Nodell, an excellent listener, who encouraged me to go beyond the first clumsy drafts; Sarah Norton, Aikido Master and counselor, who inspired me with her appreciation and encouragement; David Rome, author of the instructive book: *Your Body Knows the Answer;*

Robyn Brentano, writer and organizational leader in the world of Tibetan Buddhism; Cathy Shufro, editor and writer, who provided helpful coaching; Larry Kline, optometrist and man of great generosity; Ken Boroson, skilled architect and my Sunday-morning walking partner; Connie Bousquet, life-long friend, yoga master and naturalist; Iuliana Scheir who offers an inspired spirituality; Mo Sila, personal growth coach who saw humor and possibility in my early drafts; Dare Clubb, Associate Professor and Co-Head of the Playwrights Workshop at the University of Iowa; Conrad Kent, professor and writer, whose mastery of the writing craft and skill as a mentor inspired me to go further; violin teacher Marshall Barron, an uncompromising advocate for great music and great fun; Jane Zhang, author of the novel *Steps of the Callejon* who gave me a window into what it takes to craft an excellent book; Peter Scheir who exhibits a most wonderful curiosity and humor; Tom Scheir, Peter's brother, whose logical mind and experience with spiritual practice provided helpful guidance; and Pete Ellner, a specialist in arcane tax matters, who brings a rare enthusiasm to our meditations together and offered thoughtful suggestions about the text.

Wonderfully, I found Emily Bower who, with skill and care edited this book through multiple drafts, supporting me with her sparkling sense of possibility.

Although he is no longer alive, my father continues to spread his warmth and faith that all will be well.

And through it all, I am blessed and supported by my two children and my wife whom I love most dearly.

Selected Bibliography

Aitken, Robert. *The Gateless Barrier: The Wu-men Kuan (Mumonkan)*. New York: North Point Press, 1991

Watson, Burton (tr.) *The Lotus Sutra*. New York: Columbia University Press, 1993

Buswell, Robert E. *Tracing Back the Radiance: Chinul's Korean Way to Zen*. Honolulu: University of Hawaii Press, 1991

Cleary, Thomas and J.C. Cleary, tr. *The Blue Cliff Record*. Boston: Shambhala, 1992

Cleary, Thomas. *Book of Serenity: One Hundred Zen Dialogues*. Hudson, NY: The Lindisfarne Press, 1990

Cleary, Thomas. *The Flower Ornament Scripture*. Boston: Shambhala, 1993

Cleary, Thomas. *The Lankavatara Sutra*. Boston: Shambhala, 1993

Cleary, Thomas (tr.) *Transmission of Light: Zen in the Art of Enlightenment by Zen Master Keizan*. San Francisco: North Point Press, 1990.

Cleary, Thomas (tr.) *Shōbōgenzō: Zen Essays by Dōgen*. Honolulu: University of Hawaii Press, 1986

Conover, Sarah (collected and adapted). *Kindness: A Treasury of Buddhist Wisdom for Children and Parent*. Spokane: Eastern Washington University Press, 2001

Farkas, Mary (ed.) *The Zen Eye: A Collection of Zen Talks by Sokei-An*. New York: Weatherhill, 1994

Hanh, Thich Nhat. *Old Path White Clouds*. Berkeley: Parallax Press, 1991

Hanh, Thich Nhat. *The Other Shore: A New Translation of the Heart Sutra with Commentaries*. Berkeley, Parallax Press, 2017

Hoffmann, Yoel. *The Sound of the One Hand: 281 Zen Koans with Answers*. New York: Basic Books, 1975

Lombardo, Stanley. *Spring Comes, the Grass Grows by Itself: Remembering Zen Master Seung Sahn (1927–2004)*. Lion's Roar:

Buddhist Wisdom for Our Time, March 1, 2005

Loori, John Dado. *Riding the Ox Home: Stages on the Path of Enlightenment.* Boston: Shambhala Publications, 1999

Price, A.F., and Wong Mou-Iam, tr. *The Diamond Sutra & The Sutra of Huineng.* Boston: Shambhala, 1990

Reps, Paul (compiled by). *Zen Flesh, Zen Bones: A Collection of Zen and Pre-Zen Writings.* New York: Anchor Books, 1989

Sahn, Seung. *The Compass of Zen.* Boston: Shambhala, 1997

Sekida, Katsuki. *Two Zen Classics: The Gateless Gate and The Blue Cliff Records.* Boston: Shambhala, 2005

Tanahashi, Kazuaki, ed. *Moon in a Dewdrop: Writings of Zen Master Dogen.* New York: North Point Press, 1985

Verhovek, Sam Howe. Amherst Journal; *Candles in the Snow Honor Suffering.* New York Times Archives, February 20, 1991

Note to Reader

Thank you for your interest in *Finding Zen in the Ordinary*. I hope you derived as much from reading this book as I have in creating it. If you have a few moments, you could help other readers, and me, by adding a review of this book to your favorite online site where books can be purchased and/or reviewed. Also, if you would like to communicate with me directly, I can be reached through the book's website at findingzenintheordinary.com.

Sincerely,

Christopher Keevil

MANTRA
BOOKS

EASTERN RELIGION & PHILOSOPHY

We publish books on Eastern religions and philosophies. Books
that aim to inform and explore the various traditions that began in
the East and have migrated West.
If you have enjoyed this book, why not tell other readers by
posting a review on your preferred book site.
Recent bestsellers from MANTRA BOOKS are:

The Way Things Are
A Living Approach to Buddhism
Lama Ole Nydahl
An introduction to the teachings of the Buddha, and how to make
use of these teachings in everyday life.
Paperback: 978-1-84694-042-2 ebook: 978-1-78099-845-9

Back to the Truth
5000 Years of Advaita
Dennis Waite
A demystifying guide to Advaita for both those new to, and those
familiar with this ancient, non-dualist philosophy from India.
Paperback: 978-1-90504-761-1 ebook: 978-184694-624-0

Shinto: A Celebration of Life
Aidan Rankin
Introducing a gentle but powerful spiritual pathway reconnecting
humanity with Great Nature and affirming all aspects of life.
Paperback: 978-1-84694-438-3 ebook: 978-1-84694-738-4

In the Light of Meditation
Mike George
A comprehensive introduction to the practice of meditation and the spiritual principles behind it. A 10 lesson meditation programme with CD and internet support.
Paperback: 978-1-90381-661-5

The Less Dust the More Trust
Participating in The Shamatha Project, Meditation and Science
Adeline van Waning, MD PhD
The inside-story of a woman participating in frontline meditation research, exploring the interfaces of mind-practice, science and psychology.
Paperback: 978-1-78099-948-7 ebook: 978-1-78279-657-2

I Know How To Live, I Know How To Die
The Teachings of Dadi Janki: A warm, radical, and life-affirming view of who we are, where we come from, and what time is calling us to do
Neville Hodgkinson
Life and death are explored in the context of frontier science and deep soul awareness.
Paperback: 978-1-78535-013-9 ebook: 978-1-78535-014-6

Living Jainism
An Ethical Science
Aidan Rankin, Kanti V. Mardia
A radical new perspective on science rooted in intuitive awareness and deductive reasoning.
Paperback: 978-1-78099-912-8 ebook: 978-1-78099-911-1

A Path of Joy
Popping into Freedom
Paramananda Ishaya
A simple and joyful path to spiritual enlightenment.
Paperback: 978-1-78279-323-6 ebook: 978-1-78279-322-9

Ordinary Women, Extraordinary Wisdom
The Feminine Face of Awakening
Rita Marie Robinson
A collection of intimate conversations with female spiritual
teachers who live like ordinary women, but are engaged with their
true natures.
Paperback: 978-1-84694-068-2 ebook: 978-1-78099-908-1

The Way of Nothing
Nothing in the Way
Paramananda Ishaya
A fresh and light-hearted exploration of the amazing reality of
nothingness.
Paperback: 978-1-78279-307-6 ebook: 978-1-78099-840-4

Readers of ebooks can buy or view any of these bestsellers by
clicking on the live link in the title. Most titles are published in
paperback and as an ebook. Paperbacks are available in traditional
bookshops. Both print and ebook formats are available online.

Find more titles and sign up to our readers' newsletter at
http://www.johnhuntpublishing.com/mind-body-spirit.
Follow us on Facebook at https://www.facebook.com/OBooks
and Twitter at https://twitter.com/obooks.